AF473291

Tao Yang

Dixie W Publishing Corporation U.S.A.

Published by
Dixie W Publishing Corporation
Montgomery, Alabama, U.S.A.
http://www.dixiewpublishing.com

Printed in the United States of America
9 8 7 6 5 4 3 2 1
First Printing: January 2021

Library of Congress Control Number: 2020952285

ISBN-13: 978-1-68372-316-5

ACKNOWLEDGEMENTS

I take this opportunity to thank everyone who contributed to these idle thoughts in my life, but very sorry that there are far too many to write down their names here.

And a very appreciate goes to my close friend who stand out from these:

Andy Peter Antippas

Catalogue

Preface: Some Poetry of Professor Tao Yang

In 1957, a few of Mao Tse-Tung's very accomplished poems were published. In his preface to the poems, Mao modestly contended his poems were not worth printing because they were in the old style and too traditional and old fashioned, adhering to ancient rules of verse and folk song. In keeping with his revolutionary spirit, in the last lines of The Snow (1936) he had already dismissed the Chin and Han who "lacked literary grace," the T'ang and Sung who had "little poetry in their souls," and Genghis Khan who "knew only to hunt eagles with his bow." The traditional forms of poetry were calcified and a new generation of poets was needed:

All are past and gone!
For truly great men

Look to this age alone.

The Snow, The Marxist Internet Archive

In 1942, a few years after The Snow was published, in a wide ranging lecture at the Yenan Forum On Literature and Art, Mao made his case very clear: "Empty, dry dogmatic formulas do indeed destroy the creative mood" (IV) and "...copying from the ancients...is the most harmful dogmatism in literature and art" (V).

By the early 20th century, the fluidity of the speaking voice in poetry, unfettered by rhyme and meter, "free verse," was common among American, English, and French poets. However, in China, the shackles of 3000 years of rules were less easy to cast off, but many Chinese poets arose and distinguished themselves in an effort, in the words of the great Sinophile, Ezra Pound, to "Make it New." Prof. Tao Yang certainly ranks among the best of them.

Prof. Tao and I met at an art opening here in New Orleans in 2019. In addition to holding a degree in education, his PhD is in the study of ancient Chinese literature. When he discovered I was a retired Associate Professor of 19th century English literature, that I had taught a comparative literature course which included my favorites Li Po and Tu Fu, that my wife and I enjoyed a protracted stay on the Mainland, that we regularly visited a daughter working in Hong Kong, and most of all, that I collected Chinese scroll paintings, we became immediate friends. I asked him if he would translate the calligraphy on my scrolls for me, and one evening the next week, he came to my home, read the scrolls for me, and also showed me a manuscript with his poems and asked if I would give him my opinion. I knew by then that he translated his own poetry which, at least in my experience, was unusual. Of course, I agreed, but with a little hesitation. The only self-translator that came to mind was Nobel Russian poet Joseph Brodsky, and he lived and taught for almost 25 years in exile in the USA.

No matter who translates a text, there is always some distortion; it is almost impossible to preserve, in a readable manner, the literal meaning of a poem. Often, not even the structure can be preserved. Translations almost always fall short of duplicating assonance and alliteration, cadence and rhythm, pitch and inflection. I know enough to acknowledge the great difficulty translating Chinese into English must be because English, for one thing, lacks the syntactic flexibility which allows a Chinese word to serve as almost any part of speech.

Prof. Tao is by no means completely fluent in English, yet, but he brings a high level of English skill that assures me of faithfulness and, most importantly, readability. In my reading of Prof. Tao's poems, I found a few grammatical and punctuation issues; however, after some consideration, I decided the occasional awkward English expression should remain because I could judge from the strain apparent in some lines that it was an effort to remain close to the original. By "strain" I mean mostly the ordering of his words in the sentence--which, incidentally, is a poetic technique in English called "sprung rhythm" used to great effect by the superb poet, Gerard Manley Hopkins. I am confident Prof. Tao, as a poet and his own translator, has been true to his thought and his emotion. Therefore, the only question I can answer is, are his translations poetry in English? Emphatically, yes!

In a way, Prof. Tao recapitulates the lives of many of the ancient poets. Passing through the rigorous examination system, started in the Han period and perfected by the Manchu--which regularly had a poetry writing section--allowed a young man to achieve status as a civil servant. Very often, that meant accepting an administrative position in provincial governments or frontier garrisons far from home and family.

In good humor, I suggest that this is Prof. Tao's situation--having successfully completed his studies and passed all his exams, he was sent to the wilderness of

Louisiana to direct the Confucius Institute in the frontier town of New Orleans, far from his campus, his friends, and his family. Separation, for anyone, is sorrowful, but Chinese poets have for centuries turned the distress of separation from a family or beloved into a fine art--the poetical theme of sorrow, and the attendant grief, sadness, nostalgia, and even anger, has a long tradition within which Prof. Tao shares.

Prof. Tao's poems are divided into two sections: "Idle Thoughts: 34 Emotional Poems" and 30 Philosophical Musings." The terms "Idle" and "musings" may suggest, superficially, something frivolous, trivial, or empty of content; Instead, these terms go to the heart of English Romantic poetry and William Wordsworth's definition of poetry in the Lyrical Ballads (1798)__"...the spontaneous overflow of powerful feelings: it takes its origin from emotions recollected in tranquility." Prof. Tao's poems come from this contemplative, meditative tradition, a Daoist/Chan cleansing of the mind to more closely perceive the world around you.

The ancient poets in isolation were always first taken with the landscape around them, the new villages, mountains, lakes, and forests--Prof. Tao has already published his response to New Orleans, (along with a colleague, Guanru Yin), in Poetic Nola (2020) and in other poems of his I've read. The poems in that collection, however, are in the old ballad style, with the titles of the tunes the poems were to be sung to. But even in these more recent poems, the landscape and the natural world recur, inescapably, imagistically, emotionally entangled with the other traditional themes of isolation, regret, patriotism, aspirations, social and intellectual frustration, and, of course, love, which is handled sometimes sentimentally, with tears, and other times with the acknowledgement that relationships are transient.

The Philosophical Musings are shorter, some slightly protracted haikus, but still lyrical, personal and, again, embedded in the natural world which provides symbols, like vines and birds, for overcoming obstacles in the new environment--"knowledge gives me wings to fly," the Wordsworthian "I am a cloud," and the Bruce Lee-ian Daoist,

I am a clear
  spring
My life
  lies in
    the flow

The last 17 poems in this section have the added interest of a few lines appended, a commentary, by "An old fisherman who lives among the rivers and lakes." This figure is, of course, the hermit, the reclusive Chinese sage more often found high in the mountains or deep in the forest, and, in this case, one who has also read some Nietzsche. The poems with their commentary inhabit a rarified level of thought where Daoism and Chan intermingle. It is among these poems where Prof. Tao gracefully bears the weight of his culture and its poetic traditions and many of his poems, in both sections, remind me of other, older Chinese poems I've read. I'm certain, if I could read Chinese, I would recognize other allusions and resonances in his poetry that are lost on me, particularly because, over the years, I have read many of the same poems from different translators--think of 19 Ways of Looking at Wang Wei--but even for an illiterate like me, it is still possible to hear reverberations of sentiment and emotion within Prof. Tao's poems harkening back to the ancients. Take, as an example, not as Li Po's influence on Prof. Tao, but how both poets play the same jade flute:

The Girl of Yueh (Li Po)

She is gathering lotus seed in the river of Yueh

While singing, she sees a stranger and turns around;

Then she smiles and hides among the lotus leaves,

Pretending to be overcome with shyness.

(trans. Robert Payne)

Deep Feeling (Tao Yang)

Sometimes she will be bold

Stare at me

Sometimes she looks down again,

Quietly laugh

Artless village girl

What else can she do?

(trans. Tao Yang)

Andy Peter Antippas

New Orleans

The First Part

34 Emotional Poems

Chose tranquility prematurely

I chose tranquility prematurely
Since then, life has been very different
I am a reverse traveler
I think too much about life
Reading, listening, composing
I am in the stillness like water
Above me, there are floating clouds
Many stars and the moon/the birds and wind
Even a leaf can affect me
I tasted the loneliness like the sea
Experience the mood that best fits nature at this moment
Tears shed
No one bothers me
I am the loneliest and happiest man in the universe

Wanderer

Mid-autumn night scene is like a cup of tea
The city changed from strangely brightly lit
to a haze
Families getting together to celebrate
is my most heartbroken vision

Depressed walking alone, Depressed walking alone
Almost no noise on the street at late night
No one noticed me
My shadow
is my companion

Before me is a road
Behind me is also a road
I approached the street
And I walked away again
I will be there wherever I go
but my footsteps are never on that narrow road

I'm going to fly

I can't give you the life you want,
you are the person I love
but I will let you go
And I would like to see this world
The distant illusion is the original existence in my heart
Everything in front of me should float away in the distance
It is not my cruelty which is like snow
My pursuit is destined by my blood,
I am a leaf like a feather
My happiness lies in my ability to float in the wind
The sky is too high, the roof here broke my head
I envy the lark floating in the air
I yearn for freedom as a bird
I'm going to fly, my girl, wipe your tears
Please unlock the bird cage for me!

Untitled

The moonlight at night flows into the pond of light dreams
Butterfly resting on light yellow sunflower
Childhood memory has not faded
Today you will be my bride
Violet leaves are purple
Violet flowers like stars
There is a girl with pink color
She walked past the melodious window of my green season

My happiness

I can hear the sound of wind flowing in the sky
A clear sound like water
This guest from the far north
is sharpening my thoughts which come from the north

I walked through the wind which is my brother
Silently thinking
Since the wind was against me
I've learned to tolerate all the power that is against me
Since I'm tired of emotion
I became proud just like steel
Wind! I despise you
Just as you despise me!

When I

When my dark hair turned into green forest
When my glittering eyes become distant stars
When my proud bones belong to the hill
When my thin body was returned to the earth
My blue thinking disappeared into the wind
Then, there will be no more echo
Ringing from the valley of history

Mind

Bee, butterfly, moth, cicada
Which one is the most personable?

A touch of rain
Dissolve a love

Shore or dream?
Depressed grass
Looking for yesterday's boy

Pursue

The breath is
full of yellow sand
from the crushed land,

A team of
heavy luggage is coming over
from the desolate horizon,

The far destination
must be walking through
the long desolation,

Footprints
always remain
in the desert!

Past

Mixing the unfamiliar feeling
searching the familiar you in memory

Your flowing
Loving eyes

Getting colder gently
Like a sharp sword
Coming out of its scabbard

Commemorate the December 9th Movement

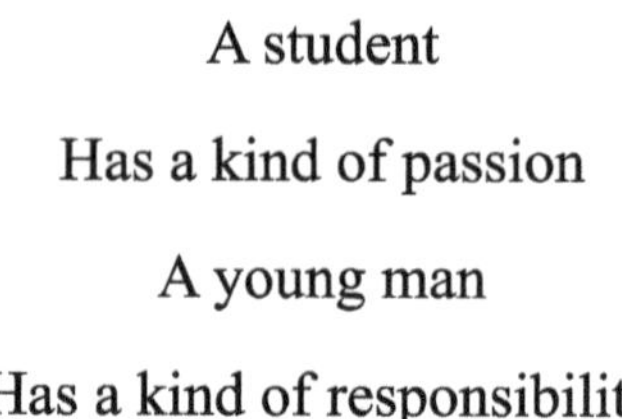

A student
Has a kind of passion
A young man
Has a kind of responsibility

The ambitious university students
Tighten the rope of the motherland's destiny deeply into their young shoulders
Regardless of the wind, the rain, the thunder, and the lightning
Also weren`t afraid of the bayonet cold as ice
Pouring their hot blood on the battlefield to
Engraved that capitalized "national soul" with their life

December 9th, December 9th

Stimulated the blood of our nationality
They fought their way out of this chaotic world
1935 catalyzed the patriotism of Yan Huang`s children
To anger like hellfire
There is a deafening voice all over China: "to survive, to survive!"

However, everything of yesterday
Has become today's history
To be patriotic is up to the era
Yesterday's students overcame their great burden
with their willpower increased by the turbulent times
Today's students have a kind of innocence about them

We innocence, how do we inherit the spirit of December 9th
when we leave the ivory tower?

The affection of my whole life

Purple flute played in the breeze
Cherry blossoms in the rain

Do all the leaves still remember?
Now that you and I are oceans apart

The faint singing voice is floating in the distance,
immersed in mist

Faltering footsteps
Wandering into sight of the scenery

Sadness left by the
window next to the street

It's not the light color of the rain

It isn`t it.

It’s not the sad flute sounds

It isn`t it.

I think of you

And you are the affection of my whole life

Deep feeling

Sometimes will say send me
A star made of straw
She will say: It is what you like!

Sometimes she will send me
A bunch of fragrant peanuts
She will say: you eat!

Sometimes she will be bold,
Stare at me

Sometimes she looked down again,
Quietly laugh

Artless village girl
What else can she do?

Defamation

I am a soaring green bamboo
Under my feet
It is a vine grass
I stretch my branches and leaves into the air
Sway, free, crazy!

I dig my feet into the depths of the ground
I raised the tentacles of my eyes towards the cloud
Lightning is not enough to frighten me
I grow up despise the defamation together!

Youth

My favorite party
Has an unknown parameter

Just like that branch of asparagus in front of the window
Slim and high-spirited

Impression

Dusty cabinet top
I found two nasty things
An old spider hiding in a blue book

Hello, little friend, what have you learned there?
Aha, the big spider let go of his hands to reveal its
wrinkled face
Its black eyes showed icy wickedness

Yes, one book
with man`s secret!

This Society

I often whisper

Unwilling to let people know

I have more thoughts

However, the result is

More people

Know my secret ideas!

Thoughts

When a leaf moves slightly,

I know

The wind is coming.

The wind is coming,

I think of you

Enlightenment from Life

Romance is like autumn fog

Birth at night

And at dawn

Quietly gone

State of Mind

I walk where I can walk
No conspiracy or intrigue can stop me
I know the power of witchcraft very well
What I do best is to jump over the walls you built!

Bring it on,
In this society you can wrong me at your will,
Let's see
who can laugh more wildly!

Lonely

If this crowd
must perish,

I would stand
together with them!

If this crowd
could have an epiphany and understand their previous ignorant state,

Then I must
perform the actions of the forerunner!

Encounter

Recalling the previous you

and

continuing telling your past!

About you,

I`ve already lost my patient.

It is not

It is not as if I don’t know what can happen, but
I don’t want that thought to ruin the peace

It is not that I don’t want to approach you, but
I am not willing to allow our emotions to be subtle

It is not that I couldn`t love you, but
There is a sense avoid any impulsive action

When the fantasy drifts away with the previous season,
The stream no longer cherishes the beauty of the cloud

From now on

From now on, I know
I have lost you forever,
We will no longer be together
Past experiences become memories like flowing water,
I close my eyes as if to see your smiling face.

From now on
We no longer depend on each other,
We couldn`t love each other
You seem to be real in my dream, but I raised my hand to
touch it and found it was all illusion,
Only one pillow to be together with my lonely self.

From now on
We no longer blame each other,
We will never see each other again

When I think of the distance between us,

Which is as far as the sky,

Tears drop down and form a pool of missing you!

Untitled

There is a tacit understanding,
Cloud knows,
Moon also knows,
But wind doesn’t know!

There is a joy,
Flower knows,
Birds also know,
But the creek doesn`t know!

There is a distance,
The heart knows,
The dream also knows,
But you don`t know!

So

I am afraid that
being far from you would trigger your discomfort,
But close to you, our love is strained
So, the dream is both imagined and real.

When we talked about love, it seems to have happened,
When we speaking of why we are always quarreling, it just seems to be for some trifles,
So, love maybe means nothing.

Maybe it's fault to go forward,
It may be bad to go back,
So, standing in the middle is right.

I couldn't tell whether it is true,
I`ve no idea if it's fake,
So, keeping silent is the best answer.

Deep memory

Although after more than a thousand days and nights,
I still feel so foreign
to this campus, with its very different characters

Because, when I see it I only think of you
But the campus without you is
like a landscape without spirit

When I came, we had fun with kabob and
roast bread at the Islamic restaurant
When I came, we had fun with a leisurely walk
under the shady Sycamore trees
with a group of people who absent-mindedly
with a silent Confucius statue like a tall mountain.
with an incredible scarlet persimmon forest
Then, these produced an ideal

Today I will go back,
the broth in the Islamic restaurant is still delicious
The waiter is still indifferent
I'll still pretend to be calm in my seat
However, the opposite seat is yours,
you are not there

More than a thousand days and nights here,
Let me know about this colorful campus very well
but it still feels so strange

That is because,
In this unique campus
There is no longer the lively you

I’ve been flying far

When I run,
You show disdain

When I rose into the air,
You merely looked up

But when you wave to me,
I can’t stop my progress

Because I’ve been flying far away
Everything here
is no longer worth it for me to stop!

Girl

Cloud's tears wet your hair
Your tears moistened my heart
Not all tears can touch me
But you are so fragile

Your long hair fluttering just like the wind
Your gentleness is also like the wind
The bitter waves of the heart`s sea brushed out my eye windows, quietly, by your wind

Random rain fell into the lake
Ripples on the calm water
A page from the past turned up in my ear
All beautiful days are cherished by you and become the blue memory

The rain bell under the eaves rang out
I pray that I have you in my life

A rock

I am

in the mountain stream

a sharp rock

couldn`t block

the pretty

flowing water like girls

The past

I had thought about you and dreamed of you
I don't know how to cool that heart

I had loved you and complained to you
I don't know which feeling is true

Keep fantasy, free my heart
Let it follow you in my dreams

Everything is short-lived,
just like smoke and clouds
I had been so lucky due to having you
And I had thought I could be with you till our hair
turned grey

I complain because of you

I`m sad because of you
Every time the wind is cold, I am exhausted

My love is for you
My loneliness is for you
How many tears of sadness I shed when you left me alone
What you took away is my passion
What you left is hurt
that I dare not face the reality

When I wake up, I think back
Everything is like the past
This world is so helpless

Untitled

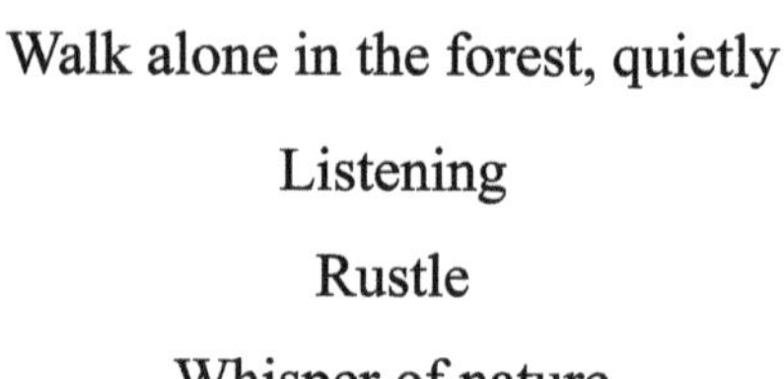

Walk alone in the forest, quietly
Listening
Rustle
Whisper of nature

That snowflake
With the weight of its life
To puncture
The air curtain

From high altitude to the ground
Sliding down
An invisible
Track

Then
In my heart

A light mist drifts past

Historical Film

Clouds disappear in the wind
Melancholy is not a sword
Only tragedy accompanied the hero

King Chu's majesty
A roar on the river bank
Frozen time and space

Windowsill

The orchid on the windowsill is open,
beautiful and fragrant
I was so moved from the bottom of my heart

You confess to me
I only share with you my calmness

I never beg, never change
It is hard for me to shed tears

Even if this love
Melts my bones!!

At that time

Your empty eyes
Glanced over
All the living beings including me

That expresses clearly
you are a person far from me

I turn around and stand on the street
Watching quietly
Slowly out of my deep sight
Your elegant footsteps and beautiful figure emerge

So I have to believe that between you and I
is the distance of two worlds.

The Second Part

30 Philosophical Musings

Encounter

I can hear

The sound of an arrow like wind

Imagination is impossible

Even though it hunts down the deepest memory!

Untitled

In front of children,

I am a teenager

Before the world,

I put on my arrogance

Explorer

Nobody wants to listen
to what I am talking about

When everyone talks about life
I have to look around in boredom.

I am a cloud

The wind is blowing my will,
Rain is washing my thoughts.

I am a cloud floating in the sky,
Growing freely in the wind and rain.

I’m

I’m

a grain of dust

which comes from the loess land.

My shape

is showing

the naive of my childhood!

Thinking

I am a clear

spring,

My life

lies in

the flow.

Childhood

I remember that
at the corner of my small courtyard
the mint fragrance

Settling among
the pages
of the breeze

Cultivation

When it's so simple that you can't see it clearly
When the proper distance becomes a protection
When the feeling becomes nothing
Well, perfect is insufficient

When you can't find your way
The future becomes distant and blurred
When the mind no longer rests peacefully
Well, happiness is also pain

When the cloud and the moon are still together
When the mountains and rivers unite as one scene
When the creek and forest become quiet under a peaceful sunset light
When I enjoy the wind and rain outside
I can relax.

Campus

Subtropical plants
Against the background of the entire landscape

Show their
Unique colors
Unique laws of growth

They can never know
How to be like the northern tree

Learn to rest happily
Also learn to grow in the coming year

Like the plants that have experienced the snow
That quiet mountain

Like the street lights can never know
What it is to be lonely at night

Vines at the bottom of the cliff

The mountain vines are growing,
The weeds around it can't bear their greatness and strength.

The vines are not like dodder and trumpet seedlings,
which are willing to entwine any host plant.

What it loves is the prominent rock and the green
pine on the stone.
That's its upward ladder.

As for the rot grass that blocked it from looking up at
the top of the cliff,
The vines disdains to rely on the rot grass and unearths
it smoothly.

Relying on their own upward force,
Leaning against the strongest stone wall,
The vines are growing !

Character

When the wind wakes me up

I prefer to fly to the sun

Direction

Follow the river,

You will find the sea.

How happy I am!

Because I have found the river.

Trace

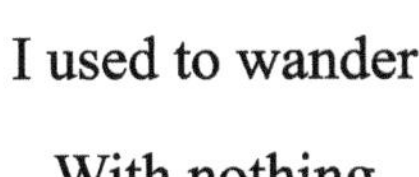

I used to wander

With nothing

My clothes are still dusty from

When I traveled on the road

My sky

The sky is my sky,
Land is someone else's land,
I swim in the air, free, floating
People on the ground smile at me

Knowledge gives me wings to fly
Reality, but it tempts me to face life

I'm not
The same as anyone!

An old fisherman who lives among the rivers and lakes comments: the entanglement of ideal and reality.

A cup of water

From the center to the shore,
The wave is layer upon layer with
The wind stroking the fine waves

There is a
Surging motion here

Zen-like,
Nowhere is quiet

But this is just a glass of water
I put it on the beach

An old fisherman who lives among the rivers and lakes comments: Only by extending the time and space can we experience the waves of this moment.

World

Professors

Talking Incessantly

Farmers

Working Silently

Two types of people

Dress up our lives in two different ways

An old fisherman who lives among the rivers and lakes comments: Each one has their own way of survival.

The Philosopher

Illusion is not always false
If this kind of statement is unfamiliar to you
That's because you`ve grown up in reality

I walk on my own way freely
Sometimes like a fragment of a cloud
Sometimes like the moon
I always stand on the highland
And put some rain and light
On the people!

An old fisherman who lives among the rivers and lakes comments: Nietzsche said that we must be lifted up—who is the power that lifts us up? It is those who are sincere, those who are no longer animals, namely philosophers, artists and saints. . . . So, people need spiritual teachers.

After Stepping Out of School

At day

I'm still awake

At night

I have to be like everyone and

Go to sleep!

An old fisherman who lives among the rivers and lakes comments: I can express only if I experience, I had to face the society after walking out of the spiritual ivory tower.

Dawn

Quiet and fresh at dawn
Like a girl with a veil

As soon as you come,

The night flees away
With its long legs

An old fisherman who lives among the rivers and lakes comments: It's just a logical feeling, but do not need to ask why.

I'm lonely

I am lonely
Just because I am tall!

The mountain pine said to the clouds which
Come over with the wind.

An old fisherman who lives among the rivers and lakes comments: It is the description in fantasy, and also the survival height of another kind of people.

Please stay away from me

Please stay away from me,
gorgeous lady

I am a piece of
cloud with thunder!

An old fisherman who lives among the rivers and lakes comments: The poet is otherworldly!

Sharpen

Being mocked, being scolded,
I step on them.

Loneliness, solitude,
I endure them.

Being dogged by bad luck
I conquer it.

Come on, my soul is smiling
Despising the space of this world.

An old fisherman who lives among the rivers and lakes comments: A strong will is a prerequisite for survival!

Homeland

I am weak but arrogant
My talent allows me to have strong beliefs!
It is not me howling better than a wolf
It is just that the people around me are still hovering in
my elementary stage

I am not interested in fame and fortune
My direction
lies in the high mountains
where the flying eagle lives!

An old fisherman who lives among the rivers and lakes comments: The powerful spiritual world.

This world

After saying goodbye to people,
I always find
mud in one hand
ink in the other

Then,
I had no choice but to be silent.

An old fisherman who lives among the rivers and lakes comments: Maybe boredom and entertainment are what life is about.

Near and Far

Hyperopic people say:
I look at the close things through glasses,
I observe a distant place with my thoughts.

Myopic People say:
I look at the distant place through glasses,
I observe close things with my thoughts.

Two kinds of people have
Two different worldviews.

An old fisherman who lives among the rivers and lakes comments: In the eyes of the poet, all people who wear glasses are patients; then, are all people who are not wearing glasses healthy?

Longing

Star,

Each star guards its own piece of darkness.

But

If the stars can come together

I laughed

What an exhausting night that should be!

An old fisherman who lives among the rivers and lakes comments: *Oh, my sun! It must be the reverie of being alone on the balcony in the starry night.*

Bosom friend

The bird carried off
my poems which were on the windowsill

I feel
happy and satisfied!

An old fisherman who lives among the rivers and lakes comments: lonely poet!

Mission

I take suffering
as my happiness
I am content with
the torture to myself
I know you
disdain it.

Sometimes I think,
is it too demanding on myself?
But I think,
I should be different from everyone!

An old fisherman who lives among the rivers and lakes comments: Principle means self-abuse, but it cannot be completely absent, it is necessary to give yourself a reason.

Life

This is a dusty net
There are still many insects` shells on it

The spider who achieves nirvana in meditation
as well as
the moths burned in the chase

If Nature allows me to choose freely
I prefer to be a little grass firefly
Flitting around in the dream sky

An old fisherman who lives among the rivers and lakes comments: People are present for specific life goals and have shown such existence, but everyone has different ideas that are born instead of that imposed or endowed by life.

The truth

I know little about this world,

But,

Many people know less than I do

So,

I become the wise one

An old fisherman who lives among the rivers and lakes comments: Contrast means that the ultimate knowledge and always-right-experts do not exist, so no one can know the ultimate truth, everything is relative.

About the Poet

After receiving my Ph.D in Ancient Chinese Literature at Beijing Language and Culture University, I was an Associate Professor at Hebei University. After that, I was invited to be a Visiting Associate Professor of Chinese Studies at Xavier University of Louisiana and also worked as Adjunct Chinese Language Instructor at Nicholls State University.

As a foreigner who has been living in New Orleans for years, I am greatly involved in the unique local lifestyle and multi-cultural community. In particular, I like to spend my spare time practicing Chen-Style Tai-Chi in the beautiful City Park under the old Singing Oak with my co-workers and friends.

During my time living in the U.S, teaching and writing

have been my primary focus in life. Moreover, it has been my wish to share my thoughts in the form of poetry. My poems capture and express my subtle thoughts and hopes as well as represent very important aspects of my life.

In this volume, there are poems I created over the years, reflecting my growth as a poet, and my unique imprints left on society. Some of these poems disclose a deeply immature part of my soul; some are intended for reading appreciation; others are simple comments in the name of the old fisherman.

My work not only manifests my interpretation as an author, but also becomes a way of communication with the readers.

If you have any questions, please do not hesitate to contact me via my email:549581080@QQ.com.

THE THEATER OF
DISAPPEARANCE

www.ingramcontent.com/pod-product-compliance
Ingram Content Group UK Ltd.
Pitfield, Milton Keynes, MK11 3LW, UK
UKHW040010200726
13854UKWH00001B/132

9 781683 723165